Diggin' Up Worms

Diggin' Up Worms

Boys Will Be Boys | R. Hal Ritter Jr.

R. Hal Ritter Jr.

TATE PUBLISHING
AND **ENTERPRISES**, LLC

Published by Tate Publishing & Enterprises, LLC
127 E. Trade Center Terrace | Mustang, Oklahoma 73064 USA
1.888.361.9473 | www.tatepublishing.com

Tate Publishing is committed to excellence in the publishing industry. The company reflects the philosophy established by the founders, based on Psalm 68:11,
"The Lord gave the word and great was the company of those who published it."

Book design copyright © 2012 by Tate Publishing, LLC. All rights reserved.
Cover design by Shawn Collins
Interior design by Sarah Kirchen

Published in the United States of America

ISBN: 978-1-61862-805-3
1. Family & Relationships / Life Stages / School Age
2. Fiction / Coming Of Age
12.04.11

This book is dedicated to my two
children, Joshua and Allison.
It is a joy for me to be your father.

Table of Contents

Getting Started

I like being a boy. Like other boys, there are things that I like and things that I like to do. It seems to me that boys have to learn a lot of stuff. I sometimes wonder how I will ever learn everything I am supposed to learn. Grown ups know so much. How will I ever learn enough to be a grown up? I wonder how Momma and Daddy learned so much.

And there are also boys who are older. I wonder how they learn what they need to know to be older. They seem to know a lot of stuff that I don't know. Like about girls. They seem to know how to talk to girls. How do they learn to talk to girls?

And talking to God. Momma and Daddy and the preacher and the Sunday School teacher all say it's important to talk to God. How do I learn to do that? I know they all say it's important.

But it all seems so confusing. Sometimes, I think just being a boy is enough.

I don't remember the first thought that I thought, but I think I remember the house on Tupper Lane. My Daddy had the house built with fine lumber and boards reaching to the sky. At least it seemed so to a small boy. I'm told that we lived by a railroad, and the trains ran at night and woke everyone up. But I don't remember that part, even though I had trouble going back to sleep. At least that's what I've been told. And I was told by a reliable source, so I believe it's true. It was either my Momma or my Daddy who told me.

And I don't remember when we moved there. To 120 Tupper Lane. Somehow, I think it was even before I was ever in preschool. But I do remember the bed and the bedroom and the two windows with screens and the kitchen and the dining room and the living room and my sisters' room and my parents' room and the screened back porch and the screened porch on the side. I remember other stuff too, but it probably isn't important right now. But there I was, born in a hospital that's no longer there. Years ago it was changed into something else. And I don't remember being born. But I was told it was in the old hospital, when it still was a hospital. And I went home to the house by the railroad tracks. And they woke me up at night. The trains. At least that's what I'm told by a reliable source.

I'm much older now. Fifth grade. So when did I start remembering for myself instead of being told what I remember? It must have been when my Daddy was building the house. I do remember the boards reaching to the sky.

But we boys do not understand time very clearly and how one thing fits with another. We just keep doing things until someone tells us to stop. That's the way it is with me. I start in the morning and keep on going until someone tells me to stop. Or maybe when I get hungry or thirsty and I stop myself.

And we boys have things that are interesting for us. For example, people are interesting to us. But we don't really think too heavily about it. Except grown ups. They are always so big. I sometimes wonder how they get that way. And I wonder if I will ever get that big. How do they know when to stop getting bigger? And why can't I catch up to my friends who are already bigger? Especially when my Momma says if I eat right I'll grow big and strong. When she says *eat right*, she means that I should eat whatever she fixes.

And we boys are always interested in food. Sometimes it takes a lot. Sometimes it doesn't taste good. Sometimes I say "no, I don't want any." But most times I do what Momma says, and I eat it.

Now my Daddy, he always figures meat and potatoes are the main thing. But he perspected my Momma. And he always says it's important to eat your greens. Greens. Greens are just that. Green. Anything green is called "greens." Momma told me one time that there are actually real names for greens. Different greens have different names. I'm not sure I understand the reason they have different names. It always seems to me that *greens* is a good enough name. As long as everyone knows what we mean when we say "greens," then why think up different names?

When you buy greens, they're all piled up together. That's true whether you buy them in the store or from a peddler in the neighborhood. There was a woman who used to come down our road in a buckboard pulled by a mule. She'd stop out in the street and come up to the door and ring the doorbell. She'd ask Momma if we needed any vegetables.

Momma would say, "What kind of greens do you have today?"

Whatever she had, Momma would buy some. Momma always cooked the greens in boiling water.

At mealtime she'd say, "We're having greens."

That was that. We had greens.

Somehow my Daddy figured out that greens are good for you. I guess I trust him as a reliable source. After all, he is a grown up and bigger than I am. And he is my Daddy. But somehow he figured out how to stop growing when he got just the right size for the new house. Momma did, too.

I guess maybe Daddy is just kidding when he talks about meat and potatoes, because he always eats his greens. And he seems to be okay about it. So it isn't like he's forcing them down or something. But I know he does perspect my mother.

It always seems to me that Daddy knows the answer to things. And most of the time, he and Momma agree on things. And Momma knows stuff, too. I often wonder how they know so much. I want to know things. And I wonder if I'll ever catch up.

Boys Like to Roam

We boys roam around the neighborhood. And we roam around neighbors' yards. We want to know things. We just want to know what's there. We want to know where the dogs are. And where the good places are to hide when playing games. And sometimes we see things we like, and we start thinking about how we might get one for ourselves. Or we just wonder why Momma and Daddy don't already have one for us to begin with.

I do remember a neighbor who had a ping-pong table. I always wondered why we didn't have one. But Daddy always says that we have other stuff. And he's right. We have nice trees in our yard. And a nice pile of lumber under a tarp in the back behind the fence. The lumber was left over from when the house was built. And Daddy is right. That nice pile of lumber has come in mighty handy many times over the years.

Whenever we have a project, Daddy says, "Well, let's see what we can build."

And so we'll go out to the lumber pile and pull back the big tarp and start picking out pieces of lumber for the project.

I am always amazed at what Daddy can do. He always seems to have a picture of what he wants to do before he ever does it. He'll look at that pile of lumber and start picking up pieces of wood. We'll go back to the garage and start sawing and hammering and nailing. The project always ends up just like it is supposed to. Somehow Daddy had the plans all in his head the whole time. Or at least it seems that way to me.

I remember the time Daddy took one piece of wood and cut a little square out of the back of it. He wrapped a rubber band around the square, and there it was. A little paddle wheel boat. Another time he built me a whole clubhouse. And every time he just had the picture of it in his head.

I often wonder if I will ever be as smart as my Daddy. I wonder how Daddy learned all those things. He told me he learned them from his dad, my Grandpa. Daddy always says that you just have to figure out what you want something to look like before you ever start. He says that's what his daddy told him. So I figure that both of them are really smart. And I wonder how I'll ever learn to see what a thing is going to look like before it is even there to see.

And we boys tell each other stuff. Sometimes it's true. Sometimes it's not. But usually we believe each other, whatever is said. At least until someone else tells us different. I remember the time a friend at school said that fishing worms are baby snakes, except they don't bite like grown up snakes. I sort of believed him. But somehow, worms just don't look like baby snakes.

I remember how I learned the truth about the worms. Them not being baby snakes. One of our neighbors had a big pond in their backyard. At least it seemed big to us boys. It was a fun place. The pond had a little island out in the middle of it. We boys in the neighborhood would sometimes go fishing in the pond. We knew who owned the pond. We went to school with the girl whose parents owned it. I don't know if any of us ever asked permission to play around the pond. Or asked permission to fish in the pond. It was in the neighborhood. We just assumed it was part of our roaming. We roamed around the pond just like we roamed everywhere else.

One day I went out in the backyard and dug up some worms and went fishing in the neighbor's pond. I caught my first fish there. It felt like a whale. I yanked that old cane pole, and that little fish came flying out of the water over my head and landed in the grass behind me. I took that fish home. I scraped the scales off of it and cleaned out the insides. I asked my Momma if she would cook it for me, and she did. I ate it. It was good. My first fish.

One time Daddy was going to take me fishing, so we went out in the back yard to dig up some worms. Being very informed by my friends, I told him we had to be careful about what size of worms we dug up. He asked me why I was concerned about the size of the worms. He said that fish like big, juicy worms. I said that you have to be careful, because worms are baby snakes. And you might on an accident get one too big that can bite. Daddy then told me that worms are not baby snakes. He said that snakes are totally different. He said grown-up worms are still worms.

It was a very informative conversation. I appreciated that he helped me understand the truth about it. I realized then that I need my Daddy to help me know what's true about worms. And probably other stuff, too. Because boys say things to each other. And mostly the things they say to each other they believe to be true. And dads are important to help clear things up. Because some things aren't true that we believe are true.

In a different sort of way, moms are important too. Momma always says that it's important to be nice to people. I suppose that's right. Boys just kind of figure it out as they go along. Some people are nice, and some are not. You have to kind of know where you stand.

One time a girl told her mother that I was not being nice to her at school. Her mother called Momma, and Momma had a talk with me. Momma knows how to talk. She knows how to make you understand things about being nice. Momma explained it to me. When she finished, I wondered how she knew so much about girls. But I have two sisters. And I wonder if maybe she learned it from them.

Well, anyway, Momma drove me over to the girl's house, and I had to apologize to her.

It was a very confusing thing to learn about girls this way. The next day at school that girl hit me in the head with a book. I told her to be nice, and she hit me again. She said I deserved it for not being nice to her. I told the teacher, and the teacher told me to just work it out. I never did understand girls after that.

After school I told Momma what the girl had done. I then asked Momma if she would call the girl's mother and tell her that the girl was not being nice to me. Momma said no, to just leave it alone and work it out. So here we go again. That's what the teacher said at school. Just work it out. Why didn't the girl's mother drive her over to my house to apologize to me?

I learned an important lesson there about girls. Momma says be nice to people and work it out. But sometimes you just leave it alone. Sometimes you apologize, but sometimes they don't apologize back. I'm not sure how all of that balances out. Even though I was totally confused, I guess that's the way it was supposed to end up. And Momma said it's okay to be confused. I guess it's especially true about girls. Being confused.

I was glad that Daddy clarified for me about the worms that day. Somehow worms not being baby snakes makes sense. And it is true. And somehow being nice to people is a good thing to do. Even girls. And Momma said it, so it must be true. She's a reliable source.

Boys Like Bicycles

One thing that is very true about us boys is that we like bicycles. At first it seems hard to stay on. But then you get the hang of it. After that you just go and go. Bicycles get you lots of places that walking takes too long to get to. And you don't have to wait for someone else to take you.

And boys like to ride bikes with other boys. Sometimes they show off. Sometimes we have contests with each other. It's like boy-size drag racing. Big boys, before they are grown ups, race cars. It's called drag racing. They want to see who can go faster and get there first. They are not always sure where they are going, but they want to get there first. And they're not supposed to tell their mommas and daddies.

Boys do the same with bicycles. I suppose they are training for being older and driving cars. You learn drag racing at a young age. Sometimes we take clothespins and attach playing cards to the rear fenders of our bicycles. When the wheels turn, the playing cards slap against the spokes. They make a clicking noise, like a motorcycle. At least we think so.

We'll go up the hill at the end of our street and pedal down as fast as we can. We are just sure we're going one hundred miles an hour on our motorcycles. We'll race each other to see whose motorcycle can get to the bottom of the hill first. As long as no car is coming up the hill, we are okay. If a car comes along, it always interrupts our drag race. I never told Momma and Daddy that we drag race. That's one of the rules.

My friend next door has a bigger bike than I have. He says bigger makes it go faster. I think I have the best bike. And Daddy says I have the best bike. So I believe him. He's a reliable source. But every time I drag race my friend down the hill, he wins. I never can figure it out. He says it's because he has a bigger bike. Maybe so. Boys mostly believe what they say to each other. But Daddy says I have the best bike. But I didn't tell Daddy we drag race. So I don't know how he would have explained it to me. So I never really figured it out.

We ride our bikes all over town. When a boy gets a bike, he quits exploring the neighbors' yards on foot. He starts exploring the town. I'll ride my bike to school on the sidewalk. Boys ride fast past girls who are walking to school. We always tell each other it's so the girls don't have much time to look at us. Secretly, boys hope the girls will look. But I don't slow down. I don't want anybody to think I want the girls to look. And I am not sure what I think they will see. Maybe riding fast is a way of showing the girls I'm a good drag racer. I'm planning ahead. Maybe.

But I sure don't want the girls to know that I always lose the drag race to the boy who lives next door to me. If they ever did find out, I'll say it is because he has a bigger bike. I'm still not sure if that is the right answer. And I'm not going to ask Daddy to explain it. But I can't tell a girl that I have the best bike. Because then I can't explain why I have the best bike but I always lose the drag race.

Friends are important to boys. But we don't talk much about it. We play together doing stuff. Just stuff. We'll play until someone tells us to stop. Or maybe til we get hungry or thirsty. Then we'll go to our Mommas and ask for something to eat or drink. Mommas are important for stuff like that.

And we boys like little cars and trucks. Little cars and trucks help us feel big in a world where we sometimes feel small. With our little cars and trucks we can make a whole town around the roots of a tree. Some roots grow on top of the dirt before going under it. We imagine the roots are buildings, and we make streets all around them. Sometimes we dig under them and make a tunnel. Roots are good for playing with little cars. When you finish playing, you just take your cars and put them in your pocket, and you're done. There's no cleanup. The roots stay there. They'll be there the next time you want to play.

Sometimes we play little cars in the sandbox in the backyard. It is a fine sandbox that Daddy made. And he put nice sand in it. And we play little cars in it. And we make roads all around it. And the sand gets all in our clothes. But I don't think I ever notice it. Until it is time to come in the house. Then Momma makes me take off my pants on the back screen porch before I come on in the house.

We have a great time with our little cars. We drive to the lake to go fishing. We drive to the school for a baseball game. We drive to church and listen to a sermon. We drag race. We drive to the ocean. Sometimes we get a flat tire, and we have to figure out how to change it. We play until it is time to stop.

As a boy, something I don't like to talk about is fighting. But sometimes boys get into fights. It's not a good idea. It's like drag racing down the hill. You just want to win. But I don't win. It seems like all my friends are bigger and stronger than I am. I don't know why. I'm willing to grow bigger, but it does not happen. Even though I eat my greens. And Momma says the greens will make me big and strong. Maybe my friends eat more greens than I do. But it does seem like I eat a lot of greens.

When we drag race on our bikes, nobody gets hurt when you lose. But when a boy loses a fight, he usually does get hurt. I remember my arm hurting one time where I got hurt. Fighting is sort of like drag racing. Boys don't usually tell their mommas and daddies about fighting. I'm not sure I know why. It's just the rule.

Boys like to compete against each other. And we like to win. It makes us feel bigger. Like boys in high school who drive cars and know how to talk to girls. Whatever game we play, we want to win. Baseball. Football. Dodgeball. Basketball. Hide and seek. Kickball. Capture the flag. Kick the can. Cards. Table games. And marbles.

Boys like to play marbles. They shoot marbles. They trade marbles. But mostly they try to win marbles. Momma always says trying to win marbles is gambling. So once again, like drag racing, I don't tell Momma I play marbles. It's called playing for "keeps." When you play for keeps, you keep what you win. When you don't play for keeps, you get back what you lose after the game is over.

Sometimes I play marbles for keeps. One friend says it isn't gambling. Another friend says it is gambling, but so what? Don't worry about it. Boys mostly believe their friends. But these friends say two different things. Momma says it is gambling. And she's a reliable source. But I made up my own mind, and I played anyway. I just said to myself it really wasn't gambling. So it wasn't. That settled it. So marbles are like drag racing. I don't tell Daddy and Momma.

I know Momma and Daddy agree about playing marbles for keeps. That it is gambling. When I play marbles for keeps, I just don't tell them. That makes it okay. Maybe. I know I don't agree with them on this decision. Boys do that sometimes. They don't tell their momma and their daddy things they should tell them. It's confusing why we do this.

Some things you just don't tell. It's the rules. Drag racing down the hill on bicycles. Fighting. Playing marbles for keeps.

But I always wonder about when I get older and bigger but not yet a grown up. Older boys drag race cars. Older boys get in fights. I don't know if older boys play marbles or if they play marbles for keeps. Making up your own mind is always hard. How do you know what source to believe? Your friends? What if they say different things? Momma and Daddy are a reliable source. But sometimes they don't say what I want them to say.

I wonder if the problem is in eating greens. Momma always says if I eat my greens then I'll grow big and strong. But I eat my greens. Lots of them. And I am still not as big as my friends. Maybe Momma isn't reliable on the matter of greens. And maybe Daddy eats greens just because he perspects Momma on that matter. Greens still haven't made me bigger and stronger. Maybe Momma and Daddy aren't a reliable source on playing marbles for keeps either.

Greens and marbles. Sometimes boys make up their own minds on things. Sometimes they are right. Sometimes they're not. Sometimes, when it is lunch time at school, I don't eat my greens. I don't tell Momma though. It's like drag racing. And I wonder if Daddy eats his greens when he isn't with Momma.

Boys Like Water

We boys do like water. Water is important to us boys. And outside it's important to know where the ditches are that have water in them. Sometimes it's for splashing. Sometimes for mud. Sometimes for animals that live there, like bugs and lizards. Animals don't always live in the ditch. But when they do, we boys have a way of knowing about it.

And we like to play in mud puddles. And we like to throw rocks in the water and watch them sink. And throw sticks in the water and watch them float. Boys like to learn how to swim. Swimming is like riding a bike. Once you learn, you've got it. Jumping into water over your head is fun. Especially when you can swim. Otherwise, it's kind of scary.

We take swimming lessons when we are little, so we can jump into water that's over our head. And sometimes there are older girls there. In bathing suits. Sometimes they don't even get in the water. They are just there. On a towel. We notice the girls that are older. And the girls hang around the older boys.

We don't notice girls our own age. And we wonder how we will ever get big enough, like the older boys. And we sometimes think the older girls are cute. But we wonder why girls come to a swimming pool but don't swim. They never get in the water. Then why not just wear regular clothes? Or go somewhere else? Why come to a swimming pool, wearing a swimming suit, but never get in the water? It's confusing.

For some reason, we don't think about girls our own age getting older. We just wonder if we will ever get bigger, like the older boys. It's confusing. That's why boys like to learn how to swim. So we can jump in the water that's over our head and do other stuff.

It's exciting to boys when an older boy at the swimming pool speaks to him. Especially if the older boy calls you by name. That makes you feel older and important. But it doesn't always work that way. Sometimes a boy knows an older boy who is at the pool. But when you speak to an older boy, and even if you call him by name, he may not speak back to you. It's like he's got other things on his mind. And if other older boys are around or if older girls are around, he may even tell you to leave him alone. To go swim. Or something. Or to get lost.

When you're ignored by someone who knows your name, it doesn't feel good. Especially if you know that they know you. They just don't want to speak to you. Then you don't feel big or feel older. Probably you just feel small. Why is he doing that? Why doesn't he like me? I like him. It can really hurt when someone you know and you like doesn't act like they know you. Or act like they like you.

But maybe tomorrow you see them somewhere else. And they speak to you and say your name. Maybe even shake your hand. And they act like yesterday didn't even happen. It's very confusing. But boys have to figure it out.

Now when an older girl at the swimming pool, in her swimming suit, sitting on a towel, speaks to a boy—that is really special. Especially if the boy's friends are close by and hear the older girl speak to you by name. It just makes you feel good. And I want to hurry up and get bigger. And maybe I go home and eat more greens. And I hope to see her again somewhere. Maybe in town. Or at school. Or at church. And it's exciting that she knows my name. And she's willing to say it. Out loud. Even in front of other people. That's another reason that boys like to learn how to swim. So they can go to the swimming pool.

I asked Momma why girls wear a swimming suit but don't get in the water. She said sometimes they do and sometimes they don't. I know she meant to be helpful, but somehow I think I already figured out that much of it. When boys wear a swimming suit, they always get in the water. And older boys get in the water. Even the ones who talk to the older girls who don't get in the water. Maybe it's like drag racing on bikes. The boys hope the girls will notice.

I don't know when boys learn to do things fast. Like talk on the phone. Or go to the store. Or get a bath. Or comb their hair in the morning. Somewhere along the way boys learn that things shouldn't take a long time. I think it's because there are too many other things to do. Just talking on the phone ties up your time. Combing your hair a long time cuts into breakfast time. And I like to eat breakfast. And I like to be outside. So going to a store and staying a long time inside and just looking around doesn't make sense.

Boys notice that girls are different on these things. They like to talk on the phone. And I wonder how girls ever have any fun by staying inside the house or inside a store or inside a mall. And I wonder why girls don't eat much breakfast. They comb their hair so long that they don't have time to eat. But eating is important.

Boys notice that girls stay in the bathroom a long time. In the morning. At school. Wherever it is, girls comb their hair. It's a mystery. Confusing. Girls say they want to have fun. Then they all go into the bathroom together. How can all that hair combing be fun?

Boys don't talk much. And they always wonder how to talk to girls. I certainly wonder how to do it. Talk to girls, that is. Girls say talking is fun. And they say it's fun, even when they don't know what they want to talk about. We boys want to talk about bicycles and worms and little cars. Girls just want to go into the bathroom and comb their hair. It's like going to a swimming pool and never getting in the water. Boys have a different view of fun than girls. And we wonder how we'll talk to girls when we're older. Do girls ever get interested in boy things like bicycles and worms? Or do we boys have to learn to talk about all that hair combing? It's confusing.

Boys Like Cars

Boys also like cars. Cars seem so big to us. When we talk about cars, we talk about what our favorites are. Sometimes we do not even know what our favorite car looks like. But we heard someone say that a certain foreign sports car is cool, so now that's what we want. We are sure these are the best. And boys talk about engine sizes. And what they want when they get older. And how this is cool, and that is cool.

Boys learn all this information from each other. Some of it is true. Some of it is not true. But we do not read books or magazines about cars. And we do not know anything about what cars cost. So what we do know we tell each other, whether it's true or not. But it's true for us.

"Taurus has the best tape deck."

"Girls like the seats in a Firebird the best."

"Orange is the best color for drag racing, because it moves through the air faster."

"Chrome wheels help the tires have traction when the road is wet."

Since boys aren't thinking too much about girls, they end up saying something like: "When I get my license, I'm going to have an orange Firebird with chrome wheels. I'll go to a junk yard and get a tape deck out of a wrecked

Taurus and put in it. I'll change the oil myself and rebuild the engine when it needs it."

And so it goes.

Sometimes we talk to our dads about these things. But in this case, dads can be confusing. Dads talk about loans and insurance and changing the oil and buying gas. Boys don't know much about these things. We figure that our dad is just trying to be confusing. Probably because boys aren't old enough yet. We try to explain it to our dads, but our dads don't seem to understand.

"I'll buy an old car so it won't cost much."

"You'll have to pay to fix it up."

"I'll do the work myself."

"You don't know how to work on a car."

"I'll learn."

"How will you learn?"

"I'll work in a service station, and I can work on my car there."

"You still have to pay for parts."

"I'll get them at a junk yard."

"You still have to pay for them."

"They cost less if you go to the junk yard and get them off the car yourself."

"But you still have to pay for them."

"I'll be working at the service station."

And so it goes. Boys have exchanged all the information with each other, and they are clear that it will all work out. Dads just don't understand.

Boys then take their little cars and put them in their pocket, pin playing cards to their bike fenders with clothes-pins, and motorcycle off to build little cities and communities around the tree roots. And they feel much better about themselves.

And they feel bigger too.

Boys Like Pets

Boys like pets. Mostly we like dogs. Sometimes turtles and salamanders and lizards. Dogs are the best for playing. And for petting. Turtles and salamanders and lizards are more for watching. And they don't learn things. But dogs follow us around the neighborhood. And they lick. And they fetch sticks. And bark. And wag their tail. So you know they're having a good time.

If a dog runs off chasing another animal or looking for another dog, the dog will come back. He knows that the boy will take care of him. That always makes you feel special when your dog comes back and wags his tail.

Dogs are fun for boys. I really enjoy my dog. Boys learn that there are girl dogs and boy dogs. And that they look different. That's how you tell them apart.

My dog is a boy. We keep him on the back porch at night. The back porch has a screen all around it. One night he tore a hole in the screen door and ran off. The next morning he was gone. I called for him, but he did not come back. That had never happened before.

When I came home after school, there he was on the porch. Momma said he had found a girlfriend somewhere in the neighborhood. She said that when a boy dog finds a girlfriend dog, he'll do most anything to be with her.

I asked her if they get married. She said probably not. I asked her if he will run off again. She said not unless he finds another girlfriend.

This was all very confusing to me. Like when the girl that I apologized to hit me on the head with the book. I do not understand girls. And I did not understand why my dog tore a hole in the screen because he had a girlfriend. It wasn't explainable. It was confusing. But Momma said that boys are like that sometimes also when they get a girlfriend. I hope I never get like that. It would be too embarrassing.

Daddy put a new screen in the door, and he didn't get angry about it. He just said that's what happens sometimes when you have a dog. And he showed me how to replace the screen in the door. In case I ever have to do it myself. I did learn something after all. But I still don't understand girls.

Turtles and salamanders and lizards aren't like that. When they get out of their cage or their box, they wander off and don't come back. They don't realize that you are taking care of them. They're not like a dog. And since they don't wag their tails, you never know if they're happy. That's why mostly they're just for watching. They're interesting pets. And they're interesting to watch. But it's different than a dog.

A dog is your friend. And your dog likes it when you say his name. He knows he belongs to you. And that you'll take care of him. And that makes him feel good. And he wags his tail. And that makes you feel good.

Turtles are fun to watch. Boys are curious about turtles. They watch them go into their shell and come out again. Some boys buy turtles at stores. But the best turtles are found outside. If you walk in the woods enough, you'll find a turtle. You pick him up and bring him home. Turtles are always boys. Boys don't refer to turtles as "her," to bring "her" home. It's always "him."

Turtles like to eat meat. Maybe that's why boys like turtles. Daddy always says that meat and potatoes are best. Since turtles like meat, they must be okay.

I kept my turtle in a box. I put some water in a bowl and some raw hamburger meat in the box. He'd eat it all up. I kept him for a couple of months that way.

Daddy says it's better not to keep turtles for a real long time. He says they like to be outside. So I'd take my turtle out and let him walk through the grass. It was fun to watch. Then I would pick him up and put him back in the box.

My sister thought that was creepy. Picking up a turtle. That's okay. It wasn't her turtle. She did not have to worry about it. She asked me why I had a turtle. I tried to explain it to her. But I never could get the words right. It's always hard to say words to girls that make sense. It's like boy words don't fit. That's what happened with my sister. I really wanted to explain it to her. But the words never did work out.

After a few months, Daddy took me in the car out on a country road, and I let the turtle go. At first the turtle stayed in his shell. After a while, his head came out. Then his feet. And finally he started to wander off.

I often wondered where he went. I let him go at a different place than where I found him. I wondered how he knew where to go. And the grass was too tall for him to see. I could see what was ahead. But he could not see. But he just started going. I enjoyed watching him ramble off. I hope he lives a long time. Turtles do that.

I felt kind of funny when my turtle wandered off. I was sort of sad he was leaving. Daddy said the turtle was not made for being in a box but for being outside. That made sense to me. I appreciate Daddy taking me out in the country to let him go. Otherwise, I would not know where to take him. And I am glad Daddy was there when I let him go. I felt better. Not being by myself. Daddy says God will take care of the turtle wherever he goes. Since God is everywhere, I guess Daddy is right.

One time I put a lizard down Momma's shirt. It was like learning on an accident. I thought it would be fun to watch it move up and down. But Momma jumped up and started to scream. I didn't expect her to do that. She grabbed her shirt and pulled the shirt tail out of her skirt and started flapping it up and down. The lizard fell on the floor and ran off.

Momma kept saying, "Oh! Oh! Oh!" Finally she stopped.

Momma talked to me after that. She has a way of explaining things so that you understand. I understood. I never did that again. I just kept my lizard in his cage. I still wonder how it would look climbing up and down under her shirt. I never tried it on myself. That wasn't a thought I had.

Animals are very interesting to boys. We spend a lot of time trying to figure out how they are going to act. What they are going to do. Dogs are the easiest to understand. But even they do things sometimes that are unexpected.

Being a Boy Is Hard

Some things are hard for us boys to talk about. Sometimes it's just hard being a boy. Figuring things out is hard work. For example, we get tangled up thinking about smoking. Boys like smoke. And we like fire. And we like campfires. We think a lot about smoke and fire.

Boys wonder why people smoke cigarettes. And why some people think it's bad. I asked Daddy one time about it. It was winter. We were at a football game, and it was cold. Somebody was smoking. I asked Daddy if smoking keeps you warm. He said no. It was confusing. Since fire is warm, and since smoke comes from fire, then how come smoke doesn't keep you warm? Daddy said it just doesn't. And that it's bad.

Boys try out smoking. They roll up notebook paper and light it. Sometimes they cut up newspaper into little pieces. Then they roll the little pieces inside the notebook paper and light it.

Boys believe that old people who don't have much money smoke rabbit tobacco. Rabbit tobacco is a plant that grows wild outside of town. Boys don't know why it's called "rabbit tobacco." It grows like a weed and doesn't look like a rabbit or tobacco.

Maybe people think rabbits eat it. But even if they do, what does that have to do with tobacco? Rabbits don't smoke it.

Actually, it looks like a weed. But somehow boys always know where it is. And sometimes they pick the leaves and roll them up inside notebook paper and light it. Boys don't always know what to do once they light the rolled-up notebook paper. Other boys say you're supposed to suck on it. But that doesn't much work.

When boys are able to, they sneak around and get real cigarettes. And they light them. And they suck on them. But it doesn't seem to work the way it does with grown ups. Grown ups seem to like it. And the fire keeps burning. Boys don't know the secret of how to keep the fire burning.

And boys don't ask their daddy's about how to smoke. It's like drag racing. That's just one of the rules. Daddies say it is bad for you. Some daddies say it's bad for you, even though they do it.

Some people say talk to God about it. What does God say? I figure if God is a mystery anyway, it's going to be hard for God to say much on this subject. At least not in words to understand. It's one of those things that boys just have to figure out. Some boys smoke when they get older. Some don't. How do you know which one to do, smoke or not smoke? If it will keep you warm when it is cold, then it seems like a good idea. But Daddy says it doesn't keep you warm. It's confusing. A mystery.

Boys Think About God

Sometimes boys go to church. Probably their parents take them. Daddy and Momma always take our family to church. Church is important. So we go every week. Mostly we go several times each week. Some of my friends go to different churches.

Sometimes boys ask their parents about God. And about other churches. Who made God? I always thought that was a good question.

When grown ups answer that question, they say, "Nobody made God."

That's confusing for a boy. We're always told God made everything, but nobody made God.

And where does God go to church? Grown ups say God is everywhere, so God is in all the churches. That sounds okay. But how come grown ups say that a boy's church is better than someone else's? If God is in all of the churches, which one is the best? Grown ups say our church is the best one for us, for our family. How do they know that?

And how did God get to be everywhere? And how did God get to know everything? Boys think grown ups are big. And they wonder if they will ever be big. And they wonder how grown ups know when to stop growing. So how did God get to be so big?

Grown ups answer, "God has always been that way."

Boys are supposed to believe that, because grown ups say that's the way it is. Momma and Daddy say it is so. And they say it is very important to believe that it's so.

And boys like grown ups at church who know their name. It's nice when grown ups say hi and they say your name at the same time. It always makes me feel important. And that's a good feeling, especially at church. Because church is important. But I also know that a grown up who knows a boy's name also knows the boy's parents. So boys try to act nice at church. They know grown ups might tell the boy's parents if they don't act nice. Actually, I can't remember if a grown up ever told Momma or Daddy if I didn't act nice. And I appreciate that. Because I probably didn't act nice all the time. Well, maybe I did. I don't know. But it made me like the grown ups around me at church. They would say hi and say my name.

Things can be confusing to a boy. I wonder if I'll ever understand things about God. It's sort of like girls. It's confusing. Except God's not a girl. At least not like the girl who told her momma I teased her, and then I had to go apologize. And then she hit me on the head with a book. But Momma said that nobody ever knows all the answers about God. Daddy says it's a mystery. But most mysteries have a way of being solved. But God can't be solved. I guess God just knows everything, and that's the way it is.

The preacher says God talks to people. That's a mystery too. God is everywhere, and God knows everything. And God talks. But it's a special language that you don't really hear. But Momma and Daddy say it's really true what God says. Sometimes I hear things that I think nobody else hears. But it usually turns out that someone else hears it, too. Sometimes God talks to lots of people at the same time. Sometimes God talks to just one person. How does God know who to talk to? One person or everybody?

Momma and Daddy agree with the preacher about God talking to people. And they say that God knows people's name. And that's very important. People feel better when you know their name. At least that's true for boys. So it's sort of special, to know that God is everywhere. In all the churches. And that God knows my name.

Boys don't really like going to church. It takes too long. You sit and sit. People talk and sing and pray and be quiet and sing and be quiet. The preacher talks. And it just goes on and on. Boys write on paper and play tic tac toe. And they try to be quiet. But it's for a long time. And it's hard. And they get hungry and want to go eat lunch.

People pray. And they talk to God. They say they talk to God even when they don't say words out loud. And God hears them and talks back to them. Even though God doesn't say words out loud. It's a mystery. At least that's what Daddy and Momma say. And they're a reliable source. Mostly, anyway.

Boys are supposed to be quiet at church. Older people know how to be quiet. Somehow God made them to be boring. So it's okay for them to sit and do nothing. Boys don't work that way. Sometimes they wonder if they'll be boring when they get older.

Momma told me one time that I talked too much in church. I was sitting with a friend on the very front row. Momma said I disturbed the preacher. I didn't notice him being disturbed. He seemed to me to go right on. I was only whispering to my friend. Momma said whispering is not okay in church. She made me call the preacher and apologize. He was very nice and said it was okay. He said he would try to be more interesting when he talked. It was embarrassing. Like having to go and apologize to that girl. Except worse.

I never did figure out what God looks like. Or how God talks. But somehow having to talk to the preacher was like talking to God. And it was like hearing God say real words. But he was nice about it. Maybe that's how God is. Even when you bother God and don't act nice, God says it's okay. Maybe God talks like the preacher. Maybe God wants to make things more interesting so we won't get bored and not listen to what God says. If God is like that, then it will help boys a lot.

Boys Like to Learn

Boys like to learn. But we don't want people to know we like to learn. So we act up at school. And we get in trouble at school. That way nobody else thinks we like to learn. And that way our friends think we don't like to be there. We assume that other boys don't want to be at school. So we act like we don't want to be at school.

Actually, we do like to learn. We like to learn cool stuff. Like about dogs and fish and turtles. We don't much like homework. We have other things to do after school.

Boys like to learn how the library works. That's because we can find fun stuff in some of the books. And some really cool pictures. And the library is a place to look around. And it's okay to takes things off the shelf and not put them back. Part of learning how a library works is learning not to put things back. The librarian says things get lost if you put them back. So it's okay to leave a big stack of books on the table.

At home it's different. At home you're supposed to put things back. And sometimes things do get lost. When you go looking for them, you can't find them. And then at some other time, when you don't need them anymore, you find them. Then you remember when you put them back. But you lost them when you put them there.

But at the library they don't get lost, because you don't put them back. Somebody else puts the books back, and they never get lost.

Boys like lunch and recess at school. That's where we learn who's in charge. We have a way of knowing who's cool. The cool boys sit together. And at recess they get picked to play on the same team. Some boys hope to be picked by the cool boys. Sometimes they are picked. Sometimes they are not.

Some boys are never picked by the cool boys. They just sit together by themselves. And they do other stuff at recess. They act like it doesn't matter. And they don't think too hard about it.

But secretly, I always wanted to be picked. Even if I wasn't. But I did not talk about it. I just did other stuff with other boys.

I talked to Daddy about it one time. I told him I was not picked, but I wanted to be. I told him the boys said I was not big enough. Daddy said everybody has something they are good at. He said I have to figure out what that something is for me. Daddy then said that I am smart. And he said that is very important. He said sometimes using your brain is better than using your muscles. I wasn't sure what that meant. But I always remember him saying that.

Boys don't like to be too smart in class, because people make fun of them. Especially if we make good grades.

"You think you're so smart."

"You think you're better than everybody else."

"You're just trying to make everybody else look bad."

"You're the teacher's favorite."

"You cheated."

And on and on it goes.

It's not easy to like to learn and to make good grades. When boys say these things, they're just trying to make somebody else feel bad. I never tried to make somebody feel bad when I got a good grade. I just did the best I could. I wanted to make a good grade. I wanted to learn. But it wasn't easy. Because I also wanted to be picked by the cool guys, sometimes. I always wanted to be cool myself. But I knew I wasn't. And lots of times I was even picked last by the not-cool boys.

Sometimes boys tell you you're trying to be a girl when you make a good grade. They think girls like to study and learn and that boys don't. When a girl makes a good grade, boys say she's a "smarty pants." Then when a boy makes a good grade, they say the same thing.

"You're a smarty pants. You're trying to be a girl. I bet your momma wanted a girl instead of a boy."

So it's hard for a boy to like to learn. You have to act up sometimes to cover it up.

Boys learn some things on an accident. One time I had a brand new face mask for going swimming. I was all excited about it. I was swimming in the pool in water over my head. And I could see the bottom of the pool. And peoples' legs under the water. I decided it would be fun to dive into the water with my mask and watch the water when I hit it. I got on the end of the low diving board and dove in. When I hit the water it broke the plastic glass on the mask. Right down the middle. It was an accident.

I did not know that it would break the glass. I took it home and tried to tape it back together. But it never did work right again. It always leaked water.

One time I saw a movie where people who had on face masks always fell over backwards into the water. As they entered the water, they held their hands over the mask and the glass. I guess that's so the glass won't break. I did not know that. If I had known it, I would not have tried to dive with the mask. I learned it on an accident. I didn't mean to do it. I felt bad that I broke my mask.

Another time I learned a different thing on an accident. We were playing with a kickball in the front yard out by the pine tree that was second base. I decided it would be fun to hit the kickball with a baseball bat. I picked up my bat and tossed the kickball into the air. As the ball came down, I took a hard swing at it. I figured it would go all the way across the yard.

I don't even remember now where the ball went. When the bat hit the ball, the bat bounced back and hit me across the face. It hurt. I don't know why that happened. I learned it on an accident. I never hit a big ball with a bat again. I only hit little balls. I did not like the bat hitting me across the face.

Boys think some things will be okay that actually don't work out. We don't know they won't work out when we do them. We think it will just be new and fun. But then something unexpected happens. And it's an accident. And then we wish we hadn't done whatever we did. Like when I put the lizard down Momma's shirt.

Boys can't always know how everything will work out. Sometimes you have to try new things. There're just interesting new ideas that come into your head. And you think it will be fun. And you think you know how it will work. But sometimes it does something different. It's confusing. Like the girl who hit me on the head with the book after I apologized to her. That was unexpected.

Boys like to learn new things. Some learning is fun. Some is accidental. Some is confusing. And boys don't know how to know what is okay to learn or when or where. You have to be careful.

Daddy probably would have told me not to dive in the water with my new swim mask. And he probably would have told me not to hit the kickball with my bat. But I didn't ask him. I didn't know I needed to ask him. I had no idea it could be an accident. And it wasn't like drag racing. It wasn't a secret that you don't tell. I just didn't know. So I learned on my own. On an accident. I learned other things on an accident too. But mostly I learned okay things.

Boys Like Music

Most of us boys like music. But we only talk about it with other boys. And we only talk about music that boys like. We don't talk about church music. We don't talk about songs we learn in Sunday school.

Boys may sing real hard at church, if no one is really noticing. But if people are watching, like girls or grown ups, we don't sing. Instead, we sort of look around and act uninterested. Even if we like the songs. It's important for boys that people not notice if we like church songs. Sometimes boys want to sing because we like the songs. But we don't sing if we think people are noticing. It's the order of things. Certain things it's okay to be noticed about. Certain things it's not okay. Church songs are one of those not-okay things.

But we boys do talk about cowboy songs. Songs about roping and riding. And we talk about car songs. Songs about drag racing and big motors. Sometimes we talk about big men songs. Songs about winning fights or winning football games. And boys sing army songs. And songs about ships.

Sometimes boys think about songs that talk about girls. And we listen to the songs. And we hum the songs. But we don't talk to other boys about the songs. And we never sing girl songs out loud. It's too dangerous. Boys think that songs about girls are sissy. And boys think if we talk to other boys about girl songs that it means you want to get married. And boys don't want to get married. The only girls who get married are older and too big for boys. So boys just hum girl songs real quietly. They don't want to embarrass themselves.

I remember a boy at school one time who said hi to a girl.

All the boys started teasing him about being in love with her. "First comes love, then comes marriage. Then comes baby in a baby carriage."

The boy said it wasn't so. He said he was not in love with her, and he was not going to marry her. The girl said all the boys were stupid and ugly anyway. The boys all thought she was stupid and ugly.

Then the boys told the other boy who said hi that he was in love with the girl. And they told him that she was stupid and ugly. Somehow none of this even made sense. It was very confusing.

It's not easy being a boy. Things that happen in your mind can be very dangerous. Maybe a boy wants to say hi to a girl. But he doesn't know all the danger in that. Maybe he does say hi. The danger only comes after he says hi. It can be very confusing. And girls are confusing.

Momma always says be nice to people. And Momma is a reliable source. But I don't know if Momma ever was a little girl. I know she was once a girl, and she was little. But even if she was a little girl, she was not a little boy. And that's different. I don't know what happened when boys said hi to Momma when she was little. I know she didn't marry them. Because she married Daddy. And Daddy was a little boy somewhere else when Momma was little. And Momma and Daddy didn't meet until they were both grown ups.

All these questions can be very confusing. So boys just have to work it out. Somewhere along the way I learned that it's not okay to say hi to a girl. But then, sometime later, it will be okay to say hi. And there's no reliable source about when that time is. And friends don't know. It's not like worms and snakes. They don't just say, "It's okay to talk to girls now. It's okay to say hi." Because then they would have to explain why it's okay. And nobody knows the answer to that. And that can be really embarrassing.

I don't remember if I ever said hi to the girl who hit me on the head with her book. I don't remember what I said to her that made her go tell her mother and her mother call Momma and get me in trouble and make me apologize. I don't think I had to apologize for just saying hi. Maybe I said she was stupid and ugly. But that's not what I remember. And that's not what I thought, that she was stupid and ugly.

Actually, I think I thought she was kind of cute. But I would never say that out loud. It's too dangerous. I only said it in my mind. And then for only a second. So I know that's not what I said to her. And that's not what she told her mother. And then she hit me with the book. It's just all very confusing for a boy. And dangerous.

I do like music. But it's much safer to like music about cowboys and cars. Music about girls just does things. And it messes up the order of things. And it confuses boys about girls. And it confuses boys about other boys, like why you have to marry someone you say hi to. But just like saying hi, somewhere along the way, it's okay to think about girl songs. And even to sing them out loud. But nobody knows when that is. And it's too dangerous for boys to talk about. So boys have to just figure it out on their own. At least that's what I try to do. Figure it out on my own.

Trying to Figure it Out

I finished the year. I did learn some things. Some things are still confusing. But my dog hasn't torn a hole in the door again. And we boys still roam around the neighborhood together. I do wonder if my turtle is okay. But I'm sure he is. Except one time I saw a turtle that was run over on the highway. He was all mashed on the pavement. It made me sad, and I hoped it wasn't him. I hoped he was safe in the field where I let him go. Besides, on the highway he ought to be able to see. But I know he can't go very fast. And cars do go fast. So it's dangerous for a turtle being on the highway. Even if he can see.

When my turtle was in the field, the grass was too high to see. But in the grass there are no cars. So he should be safe in the grass, even though he can't see.

And the preacher is always nice to me at church. And he always says my name. I like that. So I guess I didn't ruin him when I whispered too loud. He still asks me how I'm doing. And he always talks to Momma and Daddy after church. And they don't act like he's talking about me. Besides, if he was talking about me, I think Momma would tell me. Because she's good at explaining things in a way that people can really understand.

I notice I'm beginning to think more about girl songs now. I was singing one out loud in the backyard last week. When a neighbor came by I stopped. But it was fun while I did it. But I don't know if it's okay to say hi to girls yet. And I'm not sure who I'll say hi to if it is okay. I'll just have to figure it out.

I do wonder more about talking to girls. How do you learn something that is so confusing? It's hard to figure out. Momma says some girls like to talk about turtles and cars. So far I haven't found a girl like that. But I suppose it's true, because Momma is a reliable source.

I don't motorcycle my bike as much anymore. Momma always says that it messes up the deck of cards when I use them that way. But I do it anyway. Except now it's easier to just ride quietly.

I only carry one of my little cars with me now. The rest are on my shelf at home. I keep one with me just in case I need it. One time I drew a road on a piece of paper at school and drove my little car around the road on my desk. When the teacher came by and saw it, she told me to put it away. It was a good thing that she told me to put it away. And everybody heard her say it. That way nobody will think I like to learn too hard.

But I don't get in trouble with the teacher as much now. I just do my work. It's like Daddy told me one time. He said that I may be called "smarty pants." But being smart isn't in your pants. It's in your brain. And it's okay to be a "smarty brain." And I remember him saying that some- times it's better to use your brain than your muscles. I guess that makes sense. But I don't tell anybody. They'd make fun of that too.

It's almost time for swimming lessons again. I'm looking forward to it. I like the water. And I like jumping in over my head. Especially now, since I can swim. I'm glad Momma and Daddy made sure I learned how to swim. That's a kind of learning that it's okay for boys to talk about.

I remember catching my first fish in my neighbor's pond. And I remember Momma cooking it for me. And I know the grown ups that own the pond. And I remember that I did say hi to their daughter at school. But I think I figured out that it was okay, because she lives in the neigh- borhood. And I don't do it too much. But I also don't want her to ever tell her parents that I am mean to her. Because I want to fish in their pond.

It's funny how things work sometimes. Momma's right. Sometimes it really is important to be nice to people. But it's still confusing. You think you figure it out, and then some unexpected accident comes, and it's all different.

But the earliest remembering I can remember are the tall boards my Daddy used when he built our house. It was a wonderful house. And Momma and Daddy taught me many things in that house. And mostly it was all true. Because they are a reliable source.

Boys need their friends. But boys need their Momma and Daddy too. Because life is confusing. And boys need good information. And boys don't want to do anything to embarrass themselves, if they can avoid it. And some accidental learning, especially with girls, is really embarrassing. And boys don't always have good information on girls.

Boys like to feel big. But when we are not big, then we have to work it out. How to learn. How to know what's true. How to know who is a reliable source. How to know when to listen to friends and when not to listen to friends. How to know when Daddy and Momma have the best information.

And boys like to have grown ups who know their name. And who don't tell their parents when they aren't nice.

Moving On

I had a special thing happen. At least it was special for me. I heard God speak. And I understood what God said. And I found out that it's true what the preacher says. God speaks in a different way. But you still understand it. And God knows my name. And that's what made it special. Out of all the people on the whole earth, God talked to me. Somehow God did that.

I know God talks to other people, too. There's a lot of talking to be covered with all the people on the earth. And I never have figured out how God knows how to do that. But I know God talked to me. And Daddy is right. It's a mystery. And it's okay that it isn't solved. But it's special. Because God knows my name.

All a boy really knows is what it's like to be a boy. And boys just keep doing what they're doing until someone tells them to stop. Or they stop themselves. And that's a lot to learn.

Boys are glad that there are people who know their name. And who speak to them. And who like them. It makes life fun. Like when your dog wags his tail.

In dog talk that means he's happy and he's smiling. And boys understand dog talk. It's a different language. But boys understand.

And sometimes everything is okay. Just being me. A boy. And being the size that I am. And having the friends that I have. And sometimes listening to the preacher. Maybe God talking is like a dog wagging his tale. It's dog language. And you know your dog is happy, even if he does not use regular words. Maybe that's how God talks too. God doesn't use regular words, but you know God is talking to you. And God even knows my name. It's a mystery.

I think it's time to go swimming. I like jumping into the water when it's over my head. It's not scary anymore. Because I know how to swim. And that's the kind of learning that boys like. And they like to talk about it.

And that's what boys are like.